Basketball

BY M. K. OSBORNE

AMICUS | AMICUS INK

Amicus High Interest is published by Amicus and Amicus Ink
P.O. Box 1329, Mankato, MN 56002
www.amicuspublishing.us

Library of Congress Cataloging-in-Publication Data
Names: Osborne, M. K., author.
Title: Basketball / by M.K. Osborne.
Description: Mankato, Minnesota : Amicus/Amicus Ink,
 [2020] | Series: Summer olympic sports | Audience: Grades:
 K to grade 3. | Includes bibliographical references and index.
Identifiers: LCCN 2019001948 (print) | LCCN 2019013370
 (ebook) | ISBN 9781681518619 (pdf) | ISBN
 9781681518213 (library binding) | ISBN
 9781681525495 (pbk.)
Subjects: LCSH: Basketball–Juvenile literature. | Olympics–
Juvenile literature.
Classification: LCC GV885.1 (ebook) | LCC GV885.1 .O78
 2020 (print) | DDC 796.323–dc23
LC record available at https://lccn.loc.gov/2019001948

Editor: Wendy Dieker
Designer: Aubrey Harper
Photo Researcher: Shane Freed

Photo Credits: Lukas Schulze/AP cover; Jessica Hill/AP 4;
Bettmann/Getty 7, 8, 12, 19; Imagno/Getty Images/Getty
11; Rich Clarkson/The LIFE Images Collection/Getty 14–15;
Eric Risberg/AP 16; Susan Ragan/AP 20; Charlie Neibergall/
AP 22–23; Mark Ralston/Getty 25; Andrej Isakovic/Getty
26–27; Xinhua/Alamy 29

Printed in the United States of America

HC 10 9 8 7 6 5 4 3 2 1
PB 10 9 8 7 6 5 4 3 2 1

Table of Contents

Olympic Basketball

The point guard dribbles down the court. She shoots! Swish! Another two points for her team. Olympic basketball is one of the most exciting team sports to watch. This game was invented in the United States, but it is now a worldwide sport. At the Olympics, teams battle it out for the gold medal.

Teams from countries around the world meet to play Olympic basketball.

Basketball's Beginnings

Dr. James Naismith led the first game of basketball in a gym class in 1891. He needed something fun young men could play in the winter. It was too cold to exercise outside. So he tied baskets up at each end of a gym. The players scored points by tossing a ball into the baskets. Soon, people all over the world were shooting baskets.

Dr. Naismith wanted people to be active and have fun. Why not toss a ball into a basket?

These men were part of the
team representing the United
States in the 1936 Olympics.

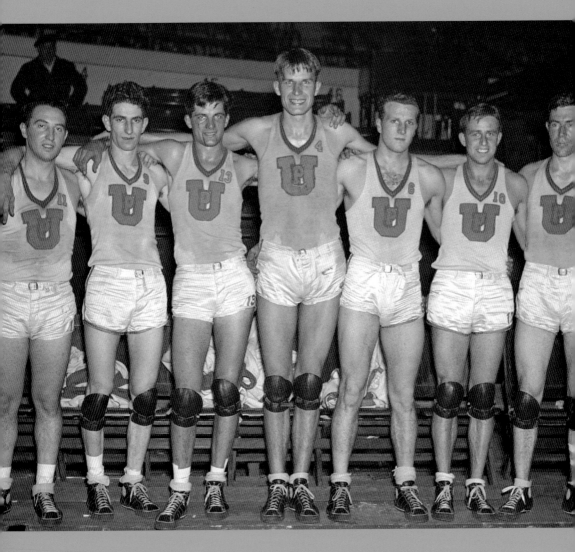

What does FIBA stand for?

Before long, teams from other countries were playing basketball. But they could not always agree on the rules. In 1932, **FIBA** was formed. It is a worldwide group. This group made the rules for all teams to follow. With everyone following the same rules, teams could easily play each other. Basketball was now ready for the Olympics.

 FIBA is short for International Basketball Federation (or in French, Fédération Internationale de Basket-ball).

Men's Basketball

The first Olympic basketball game was held in Germany in 1936. Men's teams from 21 countries played on an outdoor court. The gold-medal game featured the United States and Canada. The court was made of sand and clay. And it rained! The game was a muddy mess. The players couldn't even dribble the ball! But the United States won the game 19 to 8.

Athletes and fans fill the Olympic stadium in Berlin, Germany, in 1936.

Players from Russia and Brazil shake hands with U.S. players. The U.S. team won gold in 1960.

 Which men's basketball team has won the most Olympic medals?

In the U.S., basketball became a sport men played as a job. Athletes earned money to play games. But these **professional** players were not allowed on Olympic teams. So U.S. basketball players came from college teams. Still, the team continued to be the best in the world. From 1936 to 1972, the U.S. team won 62 games in a row!

 The United States. After the 2016 Olympics, they had won 15 gold medals.

The U.S. team's luck changed in the 1972 Olympics. The United States and the Soviet Union played in the final game. With just seconds to go, the U.S. was in the lead. The score was 50 to 49. Everyone thought the game was over. But then the Soviets scored a last-second basket. They won the game! For the first time, the United States did not win the gold medal.

The Soviets make the winning basket in the 1972 gold-medal game.

Pro player David Robinson
helps the U.S. easily win the
gold medal in 1992.

The 1992 Olympics had a big change. Pro players were allowed to play. The U.S. team was called the Dream Team. It had **NBA** stars Michael Jordan and Larry Bird. Charles Barkley and Magic Johnson were on the team, too. Some people call them the best basketball team ever. They won the gold medal game. The final score against Croatia was 117 to 85.

Women's Basketball

Women have played on basketball teams for as long as men have. But up until 1976, the Olympics did not have a women's event. That year, the U.S. women's team played the Soviets for the gold medal. The Soviets won. The Soviets won again in 1980. The U.S. team finally won the gold medal in 1984.

 Which women's basketball team has won the most medals?

U.S. player Anne Donovan fights for the ball in the 1984 Olympics.

 The United States. The U.S. women's team has won ten medals, and eight of them are gold.

The U.S. team celebrates a
win in the 1996 Olympics.

The 1996 U.S. women's team was probably the best team ever. It included Lisa Leslie and Teresa Edwards. Sheryl Swoopes led the team. These women became the first stars of the newly formed **WNBA**. They never lost an Olympic game. They easily won the gold medal.

Basketball Today

Many countries have an international basketball team. But only the 12 best teams in the world make it to the Olympics. Before the Summer Games, the teams play in **tournaments**. That's how the 11 best teams are picked. The country that hosts the Olympics also gets to send a team.

The U.S. and France battle for a spot in the 2016 gold-medal game.

The 12 teams are put into two groups. The teams play against each other. The top eight teams get to play in the final Olympic tournament. In the Olympic tournament, if a team loses, it gets knocked out. The team that wins all its games wins the gold. The team that loses the final game gets silver. A third place game decides which team gets the bronze medal.

Kobe Bryant charges past a player from Spain in the 2012 Olympics.

In the past, U.S. teams have been the best. The only year neither team won a medal was 1980. The U.S. didn't participate in the Olympics that year. Basketball is now a worldwide sport. Spain, France, and Brazil all have really good teams. Their teams include pro NBA and WNBA players. The U.S. teams have to play hard to win medals.

Spain's Marta Xargay is a pro player who has pushed the U.S. to play harder.

Cheer on Your Team!

In 1932, only eight basketball teams were part of FIBA. Today, more than 100 countries have teams. The game even has a new, fast format for the 2020 Olympics in Tokyo. Watch for **3x3 basketball**. Two teams of three play with one hoop on a half court. The first team to get 21 points in 10 minutes wins! Cheer them on to Olympic gold!

U.S. player Kevin Durant makes a basket in the gold-medal game in 2016.

Glossary

3x3 basketball A style of basketball game; teams of 3 play each other on a half court.

FIBA Short for International Basketball Federation (or in French, Fédération Internationale de Basket-ball); the organization that sets rules for basketball games played between teams from different countries.

NBA Short for National Basketball Association, the main professional men's basketball league in the United States.

professional A person who gets paid to play sports.

tournament A contest in which winning teams advance; the team to win all of its games wins the tournament.

WNBA Short for Women's National Basketball Association, the main professional women's basketball league in the United States.

Read More

Herman, Gail. *What Are the Summer Olympics?* New York: Penguin Random House, 2016.

Ervin, Phil. *12 Reasons to Love Basketball.* Mankato, Minn.: 12 Story Library, 2018.

Nussbaum, Ben. *Showdown: Olympics.* Huntington Beach, Calif.: Teacher Created Materials, 2019.

Websites

International Basketball Federation
http://www.fiba.com

Olympics—Basketball
http://www.olympic.org/basketball

USA Basketball
http://www.usab.com

Index

About the Author

M. K. Osborne is a children's writer and editor who gets excited about the Olympics, both the Summer and Winter Games, every two years. Osborne pores over stats and figures and medal counts to bring the best stories about the Olympics to young readers.